Love
on a
Faultline

CECILE RAVELL

This is a Warrior Woman Press Book
Brought to you by Warrior Woman Press
https://ravellc.wixsite.com/ravell-the-writer

Cataloguing-in-Publication entry is available from the National
Library of Australia: http://catalogue.nla.gov.au/

Title: Love on a Faultline
Author: Ravell, Cecile
ISBN: 978-0-6450452-2-2 (paperback)

Subjects: Psychology/Interpersonal Relationships;
Psychotherapy/Couple & Family; Body, Mind, Spirit/
Inspiration & Personal Growth; Psychology/Movements/
Jungian

From Sacred Contracts by Carolyn Myss. Copyright © Carolyn Myss, 2001 Published by Bantam Books. Reprinted by permission of Penguin Random House Australia Pty Ltd.

From Anatomy of Spirit by Caroline Myss. Copyright © 1996 Caroline Myss. Reprinted by permission of Penguin Random House Australia Pty Ltd

From The Thoughts of Nanushka, Vol 11: Gift of Love by Nan Witcomb. Copyright © Nan Witcomb 1985. Reprinted by permission of Nan Witcomb nanushka@senet.com.au

From The Thoughts of Nanushka, Vol 12: Tears and Tenderness by Nan Witcomb. Copyright © Nan Witcomb 1985. Reprinted by permission of Nan Witcomb nanushka@senet.com.au

From The Thoughts of Nanushka, Vol 5: Pocketful of Dreams by Nan Witcomb. Copyright © Nan Witcomb 1976. Reprinted by permission of Nan Witcomb nanushka@senet.com.au

Cover design by Cecile Ravell
Cover artwork by Anita Trevi anitac43@icloud.com
Cover layout by Ally Mosher http://allymosher.com

Table of Contents

Foreword

This book is an important contribution to our search for triumphant healing, and a retrospective understanding for those destructive relationships that can entrap us.

Cecile seeks to understand the unconscious ties that may bind us in harmful relationships and explains why so many women seem to be rendered incapable of leaving.

This is a beautifully constructed gift for so many women; those who have been entrapped, those who struggle to understand how these pairings could occur, and those who professionally accompany anyone who has endured. Thank goodness for intelligence in the little girl who was destined to survive and thrive.

Such an important book—this work is clever, profound, moving, and will help so many people.

Cecile's writing keeps the reader intrigued and empathic as she explores the unconscious elements that assist us to comprehend the classic 'bad boy' material in this tale of tainted love.

Cecile makes it easy for the reader to quickly connect and appreciate how intelligent, high functioning women can be seduced by a harmful man. Her writing is strong and real; a cautionary tale with a satisfying ending.

Meredith Fuller OAM
creative psychologist | author | media spokesperson |
film & theatre creator

Author's Introduction – The Perennial Question

Why is it people stay in abusive relationships—stuck in a pattern of behaviour until it culminates in a spiritual cataclysm? This question was often in the back of my mind during my years as a psychotherapist.

While working with one such client—who I shall call Anne—I sought to reconcile Nature and Nurture theories, so pursued a path of counselling that addressed the following questions:

Are our patterns of behaviour predetermined as part of our hardwiring—governed by our dominant archetypes (both Light and Shadow)[1]—and woven into our DNA, representing all the roles of our ancestors? Or are our behaviours learned and a product of innate personality temperament interacting with the environment to get our needs met?

Love on a Faultline is a story that observes Anne's desire to understand her twenty-year relationship with Raymond, a self-sabotaging and at times abusive man who ultimately proves unable to reciprocate her love. Throughout this narrative Anne intimately reveals and enquires into her compulsion to love, care for and remain in a relationship with a man whose childhood wounds have diminished his capacity to do anything but squander her love for him.

Anne, as the narrator, looks back on this period

of her life where she relates a candid and insightful account of the relationship she struggled to end.

By becoming aware of her role in her family of origin and understanding her governing archetypes, she was finally able to extricate herself from destructive patterns of behaviour.

Faultline definition: 'a problem that may not be obvious and could cause something to fail.'

Cambridge Advanced Learners
Dictionary and Thesaurus
© Cambridge University Press 2008

Prologue –
Sacred Contract

The essence of the fifth chakra is faith. Having faith in someone commits part of our energy to that person … As a result of our energy commitments we – our minds, hearts and lives – become woven in their consequences. Our faith and our power of choice are, in fact, the power of creation itself. We are the vessels through which energy becomes matter in this life. Therefore, the spiritual test inherent in all our lives is the challenge to discover what motivates us to make the choices we do …

Carolyn Myss,
Anatomy of Spirit

I spent twenty years loving, nurturing and trusting Raymond, despite his drinking, drug-taking, reckless behaviour and omnipresent anger. And then when he began to treat me with contempt—emotionally battering me for no apparent reason—I continued to give him love. Then, when I was at my lowest ebb, he crushed me with the worst betrayal.

A year earlier, I had read *Anatomy of Spirit*, by Caroline Myss. I discovered the meaning of the seven chakras—the energy and power they endow—and how our mind, body and spiritual health suffer when they are out of balance. I had encouraged Raymond to read it too. Sometime after, he finally read the book. It had such an impact, that he felt compelled to tell me the truth about his duplicity.

Shocked by the depths of his deceit and treachery, I struggled to find the reason behind his actions. Always a soul-searcher, I also strove to understand what part I had played in this life drama. I found guidance in a number of sources, including psychotherapy and a variety of books. The most powerful of these books was *Sacred Contracts* by Caroline Myss.

It was *Sacred Contracts* that inspired me to tell my story. I have used the Jungian archetypal concepts to underpin the structure of this chronicle. They have helped me paint a picture of our journey together.

Writing about this journey has gone some way to transmute the profound hurt and grief I was experiencing at the time. I wonder, though, if I had known the forces at play, whether I would have accepted this sacred contract.

Anne

Kismet

Women who love damaged men are destroyed in the process. These men are unable to commit to a relationship. They will drain the milk of human kindness from your body—much like a vampire drains blood from its victim.[2]

It was a chance meeting. Jacqui, a fellow scientist, had called that morning to tell me her housemates were evicting her. I wasn't surprised. Not that Jacqui wasn't a great person—she was—but she had this boyfriend, Greg. Apart from being a total know-it-all, Greg was also a 'user' who was eating, sleeping and showering at her share-house, without contributing to the household's expenses.

Jacqui wanted to come to my house and use my phone to call prospective room-letters. We phoned and got recorded messages for a few we thought were suitable, but the first one to pick up turned out to be Raymond. He was recently divorced and could not meet the repayments on his second mortgage, so he was letting out rooms. Jacqui said he sounded like fun, and he had a pool. 'He's a fireman and they have great parties,' she said, in that strong New Zealand accent I always found amusing.

Jacqui and I were like chalk and cheese, but I found her quirky. She spelled her name differently with a heart over the 'i', because she was unique. She dressed like a bohemian and rolled her ciggies. And she always greeted me with, 'How's it going, ya slack tart?'—knowing very well I was anything but.

We drove to Raymond's place and as we came down the driveway I felt a very strong spiritual pull—it was as though my soul was drawn to this place. 'This is the one,' I said, 'This is where you are going to live.' She rang the doorbell and the ugliest dog I have ever seen appeared, pressing its nose to the already much smeared glass door. A man's beaming face soon joined it. He was wearing a grey tracksuit and a stud in one ear. He wore his hair in a crew cut and seemed to be having a lot of difficulty getting the solid dog—a bull terrier—to move. Eventually, he uttered words of greeting and let us inside.

I was somehow drawn to this man. There was a magnetism I could not explain. He was obviously reckless and—from his language—not well bred, as my mother would say. As he entertained us with stories of the various potential boarders he had interviewed, his mischievous blue-green eyes kept drifting to mine, locking on and then drifting away to engage Jacqui. It was almost as if he were seducing me as he spoke.

As Raymond and Jacqui were discussing the nitty gritty of the rental arrangements, I noticed a pile of dirty dishes in the sink. I got up to wash them and Raymond said, 'That's okay, my lady is coming over later.'

To which I replied, 'I wouldn't want to usurp her territory.' Again, there was that seductive grin.

All arrangements settled, Raymond turned to me and said, 'Where do you *rage?*'

'At the St. Andrews pub. The colonial bands are fantastic,' I said. Yeah, like I was used to going to pubs. Little did he know I went just for the music, as I was not a 'drinker'.

'Well, maybe I'll join you. When are you going next?'

'Wednesday.'

'It's a date,' he said, cheekily.

∞ ∫ ∞

I was surprised at the emotions he had stirred up—both fascination and lust. What was I doing? Wasn't I the woman who, only two weeks ago, had decided that men were a total waste of space? Yeah, I said it before Phillip Adams did.

I had just ended a six-week liaison—and I knew the difference between a liaison and a relationship by then (or, so I thought)—with a total jerk; a male who used my body and gave nothing in return; neither sexual gratification nor emotional engagement. Four months previously, I had separated from my scientist husband—a man who approached lovemaking like it was a laboratory procedure. Apparently, he was so soiled by the process that he had to shower afterwards. Years later, I would learn that this was a compulsive act, induced by molestation by a priest when he was an altar boy.

I had married to escape my authoritarian father, being a slave to my sibling brothers and, let's face it, to finally experience sexual intercourse. Being brought up by a staunch Catholic father, there was no way I would risk knowing someone 'in the biblical sense'—even if it were protected intercourse—in case I accidentally brought the shame of pregnancy on my family. And so, like many women of my generation, I got trapped into a marriage—a state of *domestic servitude* to one man.

After we separated, I thought I would fuck him out of my system. So, I picked up the odd male—'odd' being the operative word—and sought sexual gratification. I never experienced an orgasm with any of the one-night stands but, strangely enough, there was one who knew how to sexually satisfy me, and that was Greg. I'd introduced him to Jacqui and the rest is history.

∞ ∫ ∞

What was this instant attraction I had to Raymond? He was uneducated, undisciplined and bawdy. My opposite, really. On their first meeting, my mother remarked he was negligent, but that was before he mesmerised her.

∞ ∫ ∞

After the rage on Wednesday night we went back to Raymond's house. Jacqui had gone to bed and I had to work the next day. However, Raymond had other plans. He asked if I liked Strauss and placed a record on the turntable. What a surprise! We listened and talked and waltzed. We kissed. It was electric—my whole being was aroused. He asked me to stay the night and I said, 'I can pick up a fuck anywhere. I am only interested in a relationship. Besides, you have a girlfriend. So, let me know when you are ready to make a commitment to me.'

He implored me, 'Can't you feel the magic?'

Yes, I could, but I wanted more than to be had. I wanted to be wanted 'truly, madly, deeply'. I drove home in the cold, frosty morning to my cold, empty bed. Somehow, I felt strong and determined. This was the man I wanted, but I wanted him unencumbered and (as I was later to realise) *forever*.

Two weeks later, Jacqui had settled in, and Raymond told me he had 'ended it' with his girlfriend. Margaret was only seventeen and he had started the liaison on the rebound from his divorce. 'Besides, she's too young,' he said. 'And she's starting to get serious. She even thought she might be pregnant and I can't cope with that.'

Soon after, Jacqui had a welcome dinner and I schmoozed around as though I was in a Robert Altman movie. All the while, I could feel Raymond's eyes on me, and every time I looked at them there was that alluring promise.[3]

After the household had gone to bed, Raymond and I were, again, alone together. We kissed, we caressed.

'Stay the night,' he implored.

'I can't. Not like this.'—The house was full of people! But I did.

What followed was a night of unbridled passion. He took me to heights of sexual gratification I had never experienced before. His desire to pleasure me knew no bounds. He was unhurried, considerate, tender. He explored my body until he found the places where his caress induced the most intense rapture. I was in ecstasy as he repeatedly brought my mind and body to orgasm.

It wasn't just a physical sensation. I experienced a closeness that can only be described as a spiritual bonding. We were united. Our bodies melded. Our destinies were inextricably linked from the moment our bodies merged. He had awakened my Lover Archetype,[4] and this was to set us on a life path that was glorious, tumultuous and, ultimately, destructive.[5]

Early Days –
Early Warning Signals

You are my friends –
my family
and all the lovers
I have known –
you are my wisdom
and my warmth,
the ecstasy
in every high
my heart has ever flown –
my pupil,
my teacher,
my eagle and my dove –
you are the music and the words
to every song my soul has heard –
you are my love –

Nan Witcomb,
The Thoughts of Nanushka, Vol 11: Gift of Love

After that first night, I could not wait to see him again. Not only did my body ache for his caress, I wanted to get to know him, to know all about him. Brazenly, I picked up the phone. 'Come to my place tomorrow for lunch?'

The next day, Raymond arrived and we ate the

Chinese stir-fry chicken and vegetables in black-bean sauce that I had cooked.

'These are the most delicious beans I have ever tasted,' he said.

I smiled.

'What are you smiling at?'

'Well, those beans are broccolini stems and you said you hated broccoli.'

'I just hate the smell of it. All we got in the boys home was boiled cabbage, broccoli and cauliflower and the smell still makes me dry wretch.'

∞ ∫ ∞

This was the first revelation of Raymond's childhood and the deprivation he suffered. I was yet to find out that he had, in fact, been abandoned in the worst way possible. This was a pattern that had been repeated by all the people he had loved and trusted. I had no idea how profoundly it had impacted his psyche and determined his behaviour. While the Light attributes of the Child: Orphan[6] helped him survive the atrocities he endured, had I understood the power of the Shadow aspects of this archetype, I would have known that no amount of unconditional love could reverse the damage that this abandonment had caused.

∞ ∫ ∞

After lunch, we made love in my bed. The same sweet

consideration, but this time with a knowing that made me feel completely comfortable and open to this man, no longer a stranger.

Over the next weeks and months, the wonderful lovemaking continued, often, usually at my house. Raymond had expressed a distinct intolerance of having people in his home and said he wanted his private life separate from the prying eyes of his boarders. Often, he would fly into a rage, railing against their inconsiderate behaviour towards their host. He started to spend more and more time at my place and, consequently, it soon became his home base.

∞ ∫ ∞

I would later realise that this was an indication of Raymond compartmentalising aspects of his life.

∞ ∫ ∞

Lovemaking was always followed by hours of talking—at which time he would tell me all about his life, particularly his childhood. I don't know whether it was his alcohol consumption or the physical closeness or my willingness to listen without judging, but he told me everything. And I listened and remembered. *In vino veritas*—in wine there is truth.

One night he said, 'You're perfect, you know that? You have no faults.' While I was flattered I did not, at the time, understand the psychological underpinnings of what Raymond meant. I did not realise that I was being placed on a pedestal from which, in his eyes, I would inevitably fall.

∞ ∫ ∞

Years later, I would comprehend that his orphan Child saw me as the 'good' Mother[7]—something he had been seeking all his life. This was an indication of Splitting—a child who is anxious over losing his mother (or 'object'), but also feels guilty because he is angry with her, is unable to integrate and see people as whole. They are either 'all good' or 'all bad'.

∞ ∫ ∞

When Raymond first projected his anger onto me, it caused me immense pain. His reaction seemed to me to be totally unprovoked—I'd suggested I take some of my clothes to his house and that we spend more time there, now that all his boarders had moved out. He glowered at me and said, 'I don't fucken want any-one living with me.'

As was my pattern, when people displayed anger, I withdrew. Disharmony was something that cut me to the quick and it was all I could do to get away from him and retreat to my house. It was almost as if he was a different person in his 'territory'. But some-how, we got over it and the loving feelings returned.

∞ ∫ ∞

I didn't understand at the time, that Raymond was displaying 'avoidant attachment' behaviour.[8] He feared intimacy because those he had loved (key attachment figures) had hurt him. He transferred his anger against them onto me. In his mind he was saying, 'You are the mother who abandoned me. You are getting too close and I am starting to care about you. You might hurt me, if I show you that I care.'

∞ ∫ ∞

Apart from his angry outbursts, a major aggravation was his excessive drinking. I had no respect for people who drank to excess, but less so when it caused them to be inconsiderate. I recall a time when I had cooked him dinner and waited six hours for him to come to my house. When he did not arrive, I cried myself to sleep. The next thing I knew it was four in the morning and he was knocking on my door. Apparently, he had gone to the Army Camp, drinking with Clive—his best mate since his apprenticeship days—and got into a drunken brawl with one of the soldiers who knocked him out cold. He retold the story with much humour and gusto, even showing me the bump on his head that he sustained sliding along the floor and hitting the wall after being punched.

He smelled revolting but still managed to seduce me into letting him come into my bed and make love to me. I remember thinking, 'This is wrong, I should send him away.' But he was so seductive, and I was so *in love*. (I now know that I was expressing the Shadow of the Lover Archetype.[9]) He wanted me and, despite all the hurt I felt, I was relieved that he had come to me. I needed him, and I needed to be wanted, otherwise I thought I was worthless. But I felt as if I had been violated—a feeling I had not had since early childhood. My self-respect plummeted that night and I wondered if I really should be involved with this man.

The next day I told him how hurt I was about what had happened the night before and asked him never to come to my house when he was drunk. I explained that I didn't expect him not to drink, but to refrain from drinking on 'our time'. I thought this was fair and reasonable and he promised that he would not do it again, that he would restrict his drinking 'with the boys' to Thursday nights. I blindly accepted this assurance, not suspecting that he was a Hedonist[10] as well as a Trickster.[11]

∞ ∫ ∞

I didn't realise it then, but the message *he* heard was, 'I want respect but if you don't respect me, I will love you anyway.' I had given Raymond permission to disrespect me. In his mind, he was getting away with it, playing me for a sucker.

∞ ∫ ∞

Not only was Raymond an alcoholic, but he was also growing and smoking marijuana and said he had used 'speed' and experimented with LSD. He had all the Shadow aspects of the Addict Archetype.[12]

What made me stay in a relationship with this man? Maybe it was my Child: Magical.[13] I often referred to Raymond as a 'rough diamond' when others were critical of his behaviour. Maybe I could see the good under the surface—like the tenderness he showed me after I had a laparoscopy to investigate a suspected ovarian cyst: he was so loving and caring; tucking me up in bed and ministering to my every need, including sponge-bathing me. Maybe I had faith in the transformational powers of love. Or maybe I was just blinded by the need to give love.

∞∫∞

The truth is, I had chosen a partner who was incapable of loving me because I did not feel I was deserving of love. Only I wasn't aware of it at the time.

∞∫∞

Love also made me lose all reason. One night after we had made love Raymond told me how wonderful it was to be with an uninhibited woman who enjoyed sex. He said he felt nothing when he had sex with his wife. She was like a sister. He was so sexually unsatisfied with her that he used to 'go' with other women when he was away on camping trips. This should have repulsed me, but it didn't because, for all intents and purposes, I understood that his wife left him for another man. He was blatantly telling me that he was a cheat as well as a liar. And, because I did not rail against him, he, no doubt, thought that I did not find his behaviour abhorrent.

Little did I know the significance of these camping trips and how they would later impact our lives.

He also told me that it was a good thing he and his wife had split up as she was trying to get pregnant and he wasn't sure about having a family. It was the same with Margaret, the 17-year-old he was with when he met me. He retold:

'The silly girl thought she might have been pregnant. That was when I decided to end it. You would have a termination, wouldn't you?'

'I'm not going to get pregnant,' I replied.

The subject of pregnancy and the possibility of having children together were not broached again, until it was no longer a viable option.

And so, I continued in this 'relationship' despite his unprovoked anger, his drinking, drug taking, disrespect and my knowing he was a cheat and a liar. I stayed with him even though he implied that I would lose his love if I wanted to have a child with him.

∞∫∞

What was wrong with me? Why didn't I run for my

life? There is one theory of attraction that says we are drawn to the person behind the curtain.[14] Behind Raymond's curtain was a bottomless empty well that needed to be filled with love, nurturing and affection.

What was behind my 'curtain'?

My Story –
Child: Magical

I had always felt loved and nurtured and cared for as a young child. However, as I have searched into my past to find some reason for all the abuse I have taken, I have come to see that life wasn't as rosy as I had allowed myself to believe. This part of my story is the most painful to recall because I realise that I had so much potential, most of which was stifled by events of my early childhood and by the roles I played in my family of origin.

I was a bright, attractive and talented child. I used to entertain visitors, singing and dancing from the time I was two years old. My teachers thought I was the perfect student, because I was polite, contributed to discussion and always did my homework. I even organised school concerts and encouraged others to participate by teaching them singing and dancing routines.

I expressed the Rebel Archetype[15] in early child-hood. Whenever my mother put me in a dress I threw a tantrum.

'Francis doesn't have to wear a dress. I want to wear pants like him.'

Another time I burped at the table and thought it was funny, as two-year-olds do. My father said that if I didn't apologise I should leave his house. I decided

I would leave but changed my mind when my less-than-loyal brother, Francis, refused to be my champion and come with me. I adored my older brother and wanted to be just like him. I used to tie his shoelaces for him and protect him against his adversaries—even though he was two and a half years older than me. So, I was hurt that he didn't 'have my back'. To make matters worse, he said there was a 'really big dog' at the end of the street and it would eat me. My parents colluded with him and made me feel as though I was 'on-the-outer'.

∞ ∫ ∞

This, I discovered much later in life, was a pattern my family had. When I realised, my Victim Archetype[16] emerged and I made it clear that I would not be a participant. This decision was to have repercussions and subsequently cause me a great deal of anguish.

∞ ∫ ∞

When I was five, my family migrated to Australia, where we initially lived with my mother's much older sister, Maria. She had a disgusting husband—he used to wave his false teeth over my food, thinking it was funny. My mother detested him—she said he had brought shame on her older sister, but never said why. Maybe because he was uncouth. Our cousins were years older than my brothers and me. The boys mercilessly taunted and teased Francis and me and their father whined about our newborn baby brother's crying. Finally, our family moved out—first to a bungalow at the back of an old couple's house where the owner carped endlessly about my brother and me playing 'noisily', then to a boarding house.

The house was around the corner from my Aunt's place and the three bachelors we shared with were very kind, but the landlord was a pig. He was always complaining about us kids and he attacked my mother, physically, when she used another tenant's laundry because our boiler wasn't working, and she had run out of baby nappies. My father then beat him up even though he was twice Dad's size. 'The bigger they are, the harder they fall,' Dad said.

So, we had to move again—this time to a bungalow at the back of an Italian family's home. They had an older son who used to show off in front of his friends by deriding my brother and me. He once kicked me so hard at the base of my spine that I could not walk for a week. Unfortunately, we had to keep living there because there was nowhere else to go.

It was at this time that an event occurred that was to impact me for the rest of my life. A mere child of six, I was abducted, with the landlord's daughter, from a park and traumatised in such a way that my tiny life would be scarred for all time. Even at that tender age, I played down the terrifying experience and numbed myself against it. My parents chose to believe the less than credible story I made up about my escaping harm, perhaps to protect themselves against the guilt they should have felt for not being vigilant. They retold the fanciful story to their friends, repeatedly, while I listened, reliving the abject horror over and over.

I never told anyone the true story. I was so ashamed. My guilt was exacerbated by the fact that my father had, prior to this event, chastised me severely for running around naked with a playmate, as children do. Coupled with the punitive doctrine of the Catholic Church, I was convinced I had somehow brought this event on myself. I was being punished. To make matters worse, my abductor had dropped off my playmate and my parents used to joke about how ugly she was and that's why he kept me, not her. My parents kept up this charade all my childhood years.

Somehow, I survived and didn't surrender my spirit.[17] Yet, I had recurring nightmares of the experience. My silent suffering is too much to retell, but, suffice to say, I developed a pattern of keeping things to myself and pretending there was nothing wrong. I recall an early example of this, which happened one day at school, when an airplane flew overhead.

The old nun, who was teaching our class, said, 'That's the Japanese and they're going to bomb us, and we are all going to die.'

At that point, I stopped eating. My mother was beside herself. She did not know what to do. After six weeks, I started feeling bad because my mother would prepare special meals to entice me to eat. I eventually told her that the nun said we were all going to die so what was the point in eating anymore. Mum 'went ballistic'. She marched up to the school and told the nun off. I started eating again but I had developed a morbid attitude regarding the purpose of living. Despite this, I lived a normal and happy life, or so it seemed.

We eventually got a commission house and moved—finally, my own room. We went to a state school where my teachers recognised my intelligence. I was so far advanced that they used to sit the 'slow' students next to me and have me coach them. I thought I was being punished because no one liked these kids, but I assisted them because I felt sorry for them. The flip side of being so far ahead was to be entrusted to teach the preps' grade when their teacher was away, just so others in my class could catch up. This, I enjoyed.

In those days, there was no alternative curriculum for gifted children, but I had the opportunity to learn empathy and also to teach little children who were a delight.

I had an insatiable curiosity and a thirst for knowledge and excelled through secondary school—always dux of the form. My parents, who did not want my older brother to feel inferior, did not reward me. They always promised him rewards, but not me. When I matriculated I asked for a sewing machine. They were aghast at my audacity, but I argued my case with my father and won.[18] My mother told me years later that, when I was two, a talent scout had wanted to put me on the stage. But my parents did not want my brother to feel left out, so they decided to ignore my talent. It seemed that my brothers were God's gift. I was just a girl, not a son.

At the age of twelve, my mother started to train me for domestic servitude. I was made to clean the house from top to bottom while my brothers played outside. I resented their freedom and I was angry with my mother for being so unfair. My father also had a cleaning job, after hours, and both my older brother and I were 'press-ganged' into cleaning a church and school four nights a week. It was disgusting and humiliating. So, after a day at school, we came home, ate dinner and then went out cleaning. I had to get up at 5 am to study, but my older brother did not bother.

In my thirteenth year my brother, Paul, was born. He awakened my Angel Archetype.[19] He was so beautiful that I didn't mind feeding him, changing him and generally looking after him. My mother was so depressed when he was born that she could not breast feed. I helped her cope. I didn't realise that she had not wanted the pregnancy. Three years later, when she told me she was pregnant again, I congratulated her. She burst into tears, but they were not tears of joy. I could not understand. Weren't babies supposed to be a gift from God? Apparently, not.

Michael was born during my mid-term exams, in year eleven. My mother was distressed because he was not feeding and had to be kept in hospital. She was accused of being a 'bad mother' by the nurses. But she had post-natal depression, which at that time was unrecognised as a clinical disorder. At six months of age, Michael was diagnosed as hyperactive—because he wanted to play in the middle of the night—so the family doctor suggested he be put on Valium. I intervened and said I would get up and play with him so that he would not have to be sedated.[20] Throughout my adult life, I continued to watch over Michael and we formed a strong bond.

In year twelve, I was accepted into an elite high school, on my academic merits. I continued my routine of getting up at 5 am to study for two hours, then I'd prepare breakfast and lunch for my father and older brother. My father would drop me off at school—45 minutes from home—on his way to work in the morning. He then picked me up at 5 pm and dropped me at the station before he and my brother went on to their cleaning job. When I got home I would help my mother with the younger children. Needless to say, my grades dropped dramatically. But I could get into teaching, if my father agreed to be guarantor for a bursary for teachers college. He said he would not take the risk.

'What if you decide to get married?' he said.

That was my only chance of getting a subsidised education doing something I obviously had a talent for. From the time I was in primary school, I had been teaching[21] other children what I had learned. I would come home and gather a group of children, sit them on the street curb and teach them the lesson of the day. And they were interested in what I had to say. I even taught my younger brother, Leon, how to read and write when he was four. This talent never left me and I continued to tutor my brothers and friends throughout my adult years.

After year twelve, I got a full-time trainee laboratory technician position and pursued tertiary studies at night. I hated the job and the way I was treated by the four female lab techs who would openly snigger about my foreign surname and make snide remarks about my being Catholic. I was on the outer, although one of the pathologists and the only male technologist were friendly. Fortunately, a refined 54-year-old Scottish woman—who had to take a job as a 'wash-up' lady when her husband died leaving her penniless—took me under her wing.

'They're just jealous, because they lack your kindness and decency. You're better than they are, and they know it. Ignore them; they'll hate that,' she said. I remained friends with her for many years and she enriched my life by sharing her worldly knowledge with me.

I wasn't enjoying my studies in medical technology, either—the only redeeming factor was the friendships I made with the other students. Those friendships sustained me throughout the following five years of the course.

Before I started tertiary studies, my mother decided to get a job working night shift. She claimed it was to earn the money to pay for my wedding, but I now suspect her main motivation was to avoid sleeping with my father and risk another unwanted pregnancy.

It was naturally assumed that I would take on the responsibility of looking after the family, as well as working and studying. So, my day went something like this:

- Wake up at 5 am and study
- Prepare breakfast for my father and older brother
- Catch two trains to work
- Go to night school
- When I didn't have night school, come home and get dinner on the table
- Iron everyone's clothes
- Go to bed, exhausted, at 9.30 pm

On Saturdays: clean the whole house from top to bottom, while my brothers played outside.

My mother used to jokingly refer to me as Cinderella. But this Cinderella was not waiting for a prince to rescue her. She had to rescue herself.[22] I guess that was when I decided that a tertiary education and a career were the only way out. But I was right, and I was wrong!

Despite protestations from my father, I left the lab job after fourteen months. I'd had enough of being exploited just because I was the junior technician— the last straw was being rostered to work all through

Easter and not be paid penalty rates. My Warrior Archetype[23] emerged and I felt strong and confident. It would carry me through a phase of my life in which I had to stand up to bullies and authoritarian people—my father included—and become independent.

I continued my studies at night school, but took a job as an actuarial clerk, at which I excelled—I was awarded three merit pay rises in two years. On my first day, my immediate supervisor greeted me with, 'I hate wogs and Catholics'.

There was no way I was going to put up with this. Rather than accept her attitude and be on the outer again, I said, 'Well, we'll see what we can do about that.'

When I left to pursue my science career two years later, she was the one who took up a collection and bought me a tasteful silver bangle. With tears in her eyes she said how much she was going to miss me as a friend and a colleague.

∞∫∞

During my time as a lab technician, I had met Mick at a dance and he was besotted with me. Of course, my parents thought the sun shone out of him because he brought his mother to our first date! What a wholesome, polite, respectful boy he was. He even converted to Catholicism. Little did they know he was desperate to get into my pants—but didn't, I might add!

They had the wedding all planned. My mother was squirreling money away and I was going to do the right thing by everyone. But it wouldn't be the right thing for me. I knew if I married Mick I would be 'barefoot and pregnant'—as my English school-friend's mother used to say. I saw how my father devalued my mother and that was not for me. No, I wasn't going to be anyone's baby-maker, cleaner and 'chief-cook and bottle-washer'. I wanted a life where I called the shots and no man would tell me to 'go bake a cake' if I expressed an opinion that differed from his. I had a vision of what women could be and would strive to be a role model to other 'oppressed' women.[24] I would not let any man control me. Not that Mick would, but my parents would continue to control me through him.

I was not in love with Mick and I did not want to marry him. In fact, I did not want to marry anyone. So, after a year, I broke up with him. But under pressure from my parents—they would not let me go out with anyone else without making a federal case out of it—we got back together again. At least I could get out of the house on a Saturday night and escape from my Cinderella life for a couple of hours.

It was around my twenty-first birthday that Gray, one of my fellow students, began to pay a lot of attention to me and asked if I would like to join his study group. I thought it was because he was interested in my mind—*so* naïve. I invited him and several other students in the group to my birthday party and my parents were appalled that I danced with him.

The following day Mick gave me an ultimatum: 'Marry me or else it's over.' It was over.

I started to date Gray, mainly because he got up my father's nose. He had opinions and my father was opinionated. Gray never agreed with him. Dad hated that. He was so narcissistic that he believed he was always right—so was Gray, as it turned out.

We dated for about a year then decided to get married. Yes, I know, I was never going to get married, but it was the only way to detach from my family without being ostracised. Or so I thought. They ostracised me in more subtle ways. My mother, who had squirreled money away to pay for my wedding to Mick, announced that I would now have to pay for my own wedding. She also refused to buy me a wedding present. As I reflected on how much I had helped her in the house and with the younger children, I felt deeply hurt, but I didn't show it.

Having no financial support, I made my own bridal dress and, knowing it would embarrass my parents, I wore 'hot-pants' for my going-away outfit and my bridesmaid wore a bohemian dress. It was a small gathering of family only—some thirty people. Although I would have liked to have had my friends come, I could only afford to pay for catering, so we had the reception at Gray's mother's house.

My mother didn't buy me a single thing for my house, but she lavished my brothers and their children with gifts. My father also did a lot of odd jobs on my brothers' houses but never once offered to do anything for me. And I didn't ask him, even though I was the one who always helped him to paint, tile and do other home maintenance. When Gray and I separated my father said, 'I never liked him anyway,' as though this was justification for him not giving me the same assistance—such a vindictive man.

The fact that Gray and I would eventually part became apparent within the first year. Unfortunately, as well as being selfish, he had revealed himself to be dictatorial. Everything had to be *his* way. He had been the only surviving child of three failed pregnancies and his mother doted on him, waiting on him hand and foot. He thought I should too. He also thought that I should do all the housework and the cooking. My interests had to be the same as his interests otherwise they weren't worth having.

I had nowhere to turn, of course. I thought that my parents would gloat if they knew how unhappy I was. I had made my bed and now I was lying in it; and what a cold bed it was. Had I known sex was going to be so boring I would have joined a nunnery to get away from my parents. After a disastrous trip overseas, we got divorced.

And so, I was finally free. Free of parental pressure. Free of the trappings of marriage. Free to shape my life the way I wanted it to be.

I knew that I didn't want to work in a lab for the rest of my life—I wanted to teach. But I had a mortgage and no money in the bank after paying Gray out. Finally, I found a sessional lecturing position, so I left my full-time lab job and found a part-time one. Then I met Raymond. I was going to be happy.

But the messages that I had accumulated in my subconscious would influence the next phase of my life. A phase that started with so much joy and promise and ended so tragically and painfully.

Was it naïveté, my governing archetypes, or was it fate—were Raymond and I *be'shert*?[25]

Raymond's Story –
Child: Orphan

Raymond was the middle son of June and Harry. Kyle was two years older and Gerry two years younger. Harry had fought in the Second World War and had moved to Moama, a country town on the Murray River. Raymond often said that the Murray ran in his veins but, as he was only four when he left, this was probably more of a fantasy that enabled him to connect to 'happier' times.

At the age of four, Raymond's father got custody of the children in a bitter divorce. Bitter, because June had been declared an unfit mother. Apparently, she would 'entertain' men while the children sat outside on the front veranda. Or else she would go drinking in the pub. I assume she took the boys with her. Why she was such an unfaithful wife was never revealed to the boys. It was easier to label her as a 'slut' and that would make her the 'bad' mother.

Raymond's father, of course, was the 'good' father.

'Dad was bled dry because Gerry was born prematurely and with a hole in his heart. While Dad was slaving away on night shift in the armaments factory, Mum was gallivanting around,' Raymond said. And, so, the story was retold, and Raymond's father was the one who was wronged. This was sufficient for the courts to grant him custody. He took the children back to Melbourne, as far away as possible from the shame and humiliation.

In Melbourne, Harry installed the children with his parents. However, Raymond's grandmother could not cope and one day she took the older two boys to the boys home, in Melbourne's outer east. They were only six and a half and four and a half years old, respectively.

'Grandma, what's this place?' Raymond asked.

'Stop asking so many questions, it's a nice place. After I speak to the man in charge, everything will be all right,' his grandmother said.

But Raymond knew it wasn't going to be all right.

'Kyle, where are we, what's happening to us?' Raymond asked, anxiously.

'It's all right, Grandma said so,' Kyle replied.

'Now be quiet, Kyle, and keep your brother quiet. We are going to see the man now so let's not have any trouble,' his grandmother said.

Raymond loved his grandmother. Although she was stern she was also warm and kind and religious. He trusted her. Later that day the tearful child turned to his older brother and pleaded, 'When's Daddy coming? Where's Mummy? Everything is so horrible. Please get me out of here.'

Kyle hugged his distressed brother in an attempt to stop his sobbing. The bond that was forged between Raymond and Kyle was to support him in the years to come. It would sustain him through neglect, deprivation, abuse and humiliation. This sensitive, feeling boy would have to develop defences to survive the horror of what was tantamount to a concentration camp for a little child.

∞ ∫ ∞

On Raymond's first Christmas, his mother visited with a big box of toys for the boys. His father took it away. Harry only let them choose one toy and the rest were given away. Raymond chose a pocketknife and his life-long attachment to pocket knives began. His mother never visited again.

∞ ∫ ∞

When Raymond was about six, he suffered a bout of dysentery—not uncommon in institutionalised children. 'The Keeper'—as the children called him behind his back—punished him mercilessly when he lost control of his bowels. This experience was so terrifying and humiliating that Raymond would later write fourteen foolscap pages reliving the horror and the torment.

To say this traumatised Raymond is an under-statement. A defenceless child castigated in front of his dormitory 'inmates' is one thing. But what fol-lowed is unconscionable. The child was sick, small and vulnerable. He needed caring and nurturing. But, instead, The Keeper dragged him by his hair, called him a 'filthy little beast' and flung him into the centre of the room—all under the watchful eyes of the other wards. He then bashed him about the head and threw him, face first, into the mess he had made in the bed. Raymond was then pushed into the shower and the cold water turned on. He endured further humiliation when he was made to wash his sheets and hang them out for all to see. After this incident, the other children ostracised him and the school bully would punch him in the stomach whenever he got the chance.

During the entire episode, he was never seen by a doctor, nor given any medication. Not only were his needs neglected by the institution, but he also felt abandoned by God. He had prayed to be relieved of the painful stomach cramps, to be spared the sneering of the other boys, to be protected from the abuse of the school bully, for his mother to find him, his father to come and for Kyle to protect him. But they all abandoned him. It was at this pivotal point in his life that he became self-reliant. He was to become the tough, fearless rebel, guarding other vulnerable boys from bullies.

While the Bully Archetype[26] protected Raymond in this hostile environment, it also transformed him into a verbally and physically abusive adolescent[27]— which masked his inner feelings of worthlessness. This episode was to shape much of his subconscious processing of perceived humiliation.

During the following years his father never once came to see the boys on their birthdays, nor did he take them home for Christmas. They were 'left to rot' in the boys home. Sometimes they were lucky enough to be fostered for school holidays, but there was no sense of family.

Finally, after eight years, the brothers were told that they were going home. Harry had met and married Iris. At last, a proper family. But, alas, it was not to be. Both Harry and Iris were alcoholics. They fought bitterly. Raymond would sneak out of his bedroom window and run as far away from this distressing behaviour as he could. And so a pattern of 'running away', the Shadow side of the Hero Archetype,[28] was set in place.

Iris was far from the 'good' mother. She made the boys buy their own milk and rationed out food. When Harry came home she would 'whinge until he gave the source of her irritation a good thumping'. Usually it was Gerry. Both Raymond and Kyle despised her until the day she died.

Raymond revealed, in one of his drunken moments, that he had fucked his stepsister when he was fifteen. Whether he did it out of sheer spite against Iris, or because he was a reprobate, I will never know.

When Raymond was eighteen he and Gerry set out in search of their mother.[29] They found her in Echuca. She had re-married and had two sons, Josh and Mark, who were eight and six years old respectively. All she kept talking about was Kyle, her first born, who had no desire to find his mother and had not come.

Raymond recounted to me how devastated he felt that his effort to find his mother had not even been acknowledged by her. Despite feeling rejected by his mother, Raymond continued to visit her at least twice a year. And when, after he was married, she was diagnosed with cervical cancer, he took her into his home when she came to Melbourne for her chemotherapy. I don't know if it was his wife's benevolence or his, but I think it was his.

As a youth, Raymond excelled at sport. He made his mark in lacrosse, tennis, basketball, cricket and played for the under-19s in a major league football. And yet he abused his body with alcohol and drugs. He also mutilated his body with tattoos.

When I asked him why he got the tattoos he said, 'To feel the pain.' His 'defended-self'—the impenetrable disguise which masked his wounded child—wanted to project the appearance of being strong and able to tolerate hurt without wincing.

Raymond married when he was twenty-one. As much to get out of the 'family' home, as well as to appease his wife's mother who was fearful that his recklessness would result in a pregnancy out of wedlock. His wife gave him a stipend of five dollars a week for smokes and beer. She managed the money and squirreled enough away for a deposit on the house.

'That's when everything went wrong,' Raymond said, 'when we moved into this house. It is cursed. She totally took me to the cleaners when she divorced me, and now I have this double mortgage. She was the one who cheated on me. How unfair is that? I blame the blood-sucking solicitors.'

And so, Raymond was again abandoned. It seemed everyone he had ever loved had wounded him deeply.

Our Story –
Star-Crossed Lovers

And so, the Child: Magical—in her innocence—took the Child: Orphan under her wing. She spun a protective cocoon around him and filled it with love. She took the brunt of all the suppressed anger that he felt against his mother, his father, grandmother, Kyle, his wife and God. Indeed, all the people who had ever abandoned him. She did this out of her innate goodness, little knowing that all the love in the world could not fill the void of neglect, nor wash away the tears of despair from his heart.

But, as it turned out, the Child: Orphan was no Oliver Twist—more like the Artful Dodger on his Light side and Bill Sykes on his Shadow side.[30]

I find it hard to tell our story. I don't know what kept me loving him. I guess knowing that he needed love, and I was eager to give it, was enough. He would say things to me like, 'We have mated for life' and, 'We will never win Tattslotto because we used up all our good luck when we met each other.' Strangely, I felt the same way.

In amongst the bouts of anger, I like to believe there was love and caring. We had a lot of adventures together, travelling around Australia and to Canada. I encouraged Raymond to believe he could attain his fitness once more and, with a lot of hard work and determination, he did. He was able to compete in Canada as a triathlete.

When I decided to return to tertiary study, he supported me by having dinner on the table every night. Recalling this makes me cry for the sweetness of it all. There were so many times when he told me how proud he was of my accomplishments. He journeyed with me over some very rocky emotional terrain and, in the early days, I always felt he was there for me—even when he really wasn't.

Finally, there was a time that I felt he had joined with me; that he was now a responsible adult. He pledged that he would commit himself to our relationship. He said, 'You are the most important thing in the world to me.'

And then, in one short year, that all changed. But, I'm getting ahead of myself! Let's go back a few years to a time when two planets, which were moving in two disparate orbits, collided! Professional, cultured—yet naïve—confident woman with a successful career as a scientist and lecturer meets penniless, uneducated (but nonetheless talented), larrikin who possesses rat-cunning. Some would see this as recipe for disaster, but not me—the Child: Magical.[31]

To love so unconditionally and to give so selflessly; surely this sets a solid foundation for trust, devotion and loyalty. When you are in love, it seems you project your qualities on to the object of your affection and you are oblivious to his flaws. At some level, there is a knowing. Maybe it is housed in the subconscious, but it vibrates at a lower emotional level than the crashing tide of the passion that is love.

However, there was a complementarity—the needy and the nurturer,[32] the child and the mother.[33] This is what kept the bond strong. Somehow this diamond-in-the-rough became my project and engaged my Teacher Archetype.[34] Unwittingly, I was drawn into his orbit and, equally unwittingly, I tried to change it—albeit unconsciously.

Always the accommodator, I became a passive pawn in his world. I watched—though didn't participate in—his hedonistic[35] lifestyle. I sat with him in beer gardens; accompanied him on fishing trips and camping trips, early in the relationship; tolerated his gambling; and accepted his social circle of drunks, marihuana chuffers, bogans and lowbrows. All the while nourishing and loving him.

Then, over time, Raymond began to change— outwardly, that is. He ostensibly embraced my lifestyle, which included: accompanying me to the symphony; travelling nationally and internationally with me; dressing fashionably and suitably for whatever the occasion; adopting a healthy diet; and following my financial advice, which enabled him to pay off his mortgage 15 years earlier than the term.

As I said, Raymond lashed out at me with a vengeance, whenever I suggested we go to his house.[36] So, I spent less and less time there until I didn't bother going at all. He even refrained from drinking himself into a stupor when we were together. All was blissful for about six years, but this period was literally the calm before the storm.

We spent Thursday nights apart each week—as well as the two nights Raymond was on night shift. He said he wanted to spend a night on his own, at his house, just to collect the mail and 'tidy-up a bit'. I knew that on these nights he would have what he described as 'a quiet drink' at home with Clive, but I saw this as an innocent pastime. Little did I know that he was pursuing his established lifestyle when he spent time at his house, as well as when he went camping.

For many years I had used the 'night off' to catch up with friends—going to dinner, the movies or to hear live music. But they had distanced themselves from me after observing Raymond's behaviour when he drank—now I see they felt embarrassed for me. I also lost Jacqui as a friend because I didn't believe her when she said she suspected that Raymond was not being faithful. When I told him, he said that she had tried to come onto him and that he rejected her. *Mea culpa*—I chose to believe him.

So, our night apart had become an opportunity for my brother, Michael, and me to spend some quality time together away from the machinations of our controlling family. Michael and I were very close—I had 'had his back' since he was a baby and, as a child, he would always run to me when he needed comforting and reassurance.

On one Thursday night at about 4 am the phone rang. It was Raymond.

'I'm in deep shit, you've got to come and get me,' he cried in a hysterical voice.

'What's going on?' I said, through a sleep haze.

'That bastard, chicken-shit Clive, has driven off and deserted me. You've got to come and get me. But first give Kyle a call and tell him to get to my place and remove the power tools from my shed.'

'What are you talking about?'

'There are some tools a mate gave me and I think they're hot!'

'My God, Raymond, what do you mean?'

'Just do it, babe, please; otherwise I will go to jail.'

'What's happened? Why would anyone search your property anyway?'

'Because the cops are chasing us.'

I couldn't believe what I'd just heard. What was going on? There must be some mistake. Was this a nightmare I was having?

'Why would they be chasing you?'

'Oh, babe, I'm so sorry. We've done a really stupid thing. We were having a drink and bullshitting about going fishing and Gazz said, 'It would be great if we had a boat', and he knew where there was one leaning on a back fence and we drove there. But some bastard saw us and rang the cops. Clive ran away and he and Gazz just drove off and left me. I'm stranded out in the sticks. I need you to save me, babe.'

I hung up the phone. Michael had now woken and was standing by my side.

'What is it? Why are you shaking? What's happened?'

'It's Raymond. He's running from the police and he's stranded without a car. Bastard!'

'We have to go and get him,' my loyal brother exclaimed.

Raymond was Michael's hero. He saw Raymond as a rugged male role model—he called him Macho Man.

Fuck him, my alter ego screamed at me to say. 'Why should I? He's a liar and a thief. Why would I risk compromising myself for him?'

'You have to Sis. You just have to.'

Against my better judgement, I hurriedly dressed, and Michael did too. We drove towards the western suburbs into the bleak and wintry night. My heart was as frosty as the weather outside. My mind still unable to comprehend the deception. I was resolute—I would get him out of this and then cut him out of my life. There was now a chasm in my heart where the well of love had been. He wanted the free life with his friends. He could have it. At this point I could have changed my pattern. Being inconsiderate and disrespectful was one thing, a lack of integrity was another. I held this value above all others and in my life had always gravitated towards people who did the same.

We arrived at the phone box to find a very frightened individual. Gone was the macho man and in his place a quivering excuse for a human being.

'Thanks, babe. You saved my life,' he fawned.

'Don't thank me, thank Michael. If he hadn't begged me to come and get you, I would have let you fend for yourself. How dare you involve me in your nefarious behaviour? How dare you?'

I was outraged. The bile kept pouring out of me. And Raymond just sat there and looked sheepish. This was a side of him I had never seen. Raymond was scared. But who or what was he scared of? Was it me? This was a side of me he had never seen.

∞ ∫ ∞

How was I to know that his defended-self was this whimpering, motherless, abandoned child? Up to that point I had only seen the swaggering, self-confident man's man; the aggressive alpha male.

∞ ∫ ∞

I dropped Raymond at his house and Michael and I travelled back to mine; in silence.

The next morning, the shit had hit the fan. Clive and Gazz had been caught by the police and 'spilled their guts', as Raymond later said. He was arrested and again called me to bail him out. The guy just didn't get it! But he implored me. 'I need your help. If I'm convicted, I'll lose my job and my house. You've got to help me.'

And help him I did. My father had a lawyer colleague and he enlisted him to plead Raymond's case. Because my father appeared as a character witness— he thought Raymond was a 'good man', principally because Raymond was always respectful towards him and never argued with him; thus, stroking my father's narcissistic ego[37]—Raymond and his 'mates' had their wrists slapped with a hefty donation to the poor box. A conviction was not recorded and they were placed on probation for one year. No one ever knew of their folly except my whole family! He hadn't fallen from grace, because he was so repentant—*good act, Raymond!*—but I had. Some of my family were sniggering behind their hands. The 'good' daughter was now tarnished for life. Michael remained loyal to me and to Raymond. He did not join in their deprecating behaviour.

This was a deal-breaker. I didn't want this liar in my life and I told him so. He cried and cried but I was adamant, until my mother begged me to forgive him. My mother had terminal cancer and I thought she didn't need to have any more grief in her life. She had been charmed into believing Raymond was a good person because he never showed his other persona in front of my family; and I wasn't about to destroy her illusion. However, the determining factor, in the end, was the fact that I loved him, and I needed him—fool that I was. He promised he would never do anything like that again and he would limit himself to two drinks so that he would always be 'in control'. I believed him. *Idiot!*

My mother passed away the following year and I had to get away from my family in general, and my father, in particular. Raymond was supportive and came with me to Canada to see my cousins and Dad's sister, and then to New York, to see my mother's sister.

I felt he was my champion. After all, I was in the midst of an emotional tempest and he was there—a rock to cling to. But something happened 'on the way to the forum' as it were.

I had previously proffered a research paper to conference organisers in Hamilton, Ontario, and so made a side trip on the way to New York, after having visited my Canadian cousins. We were catching a tram to McMaster University student housing when it started to rain heavily. We both got soaked but, while I took it in my stride, Raymond went completely ballistic and took his inexplicable rage out on me.

So deep were the wounds inflicted by his incarceration in the boys home that the slightest reminder of any discomforting situation would send him into a frenzy. He perhaps equated this chilling to the bone as akin to the time he was thrown into a cold shower when he had dysentery.

I had no idea what I had done, but felt guilty anyway, and tried my hardest to placate him. As I mentioned previously, this pattern was a common one and had been repeated over and over. I was devastated, yet again. By the time we arrived in New York there was no sign of this angry persona. It never, ever, showed up when we were with my family or circle of friends.

∞ ∫ ∞

I learned some time later that childhood trauma could lead to a dissociative disorder. Whether this was the case with Raymond, I am not qualified to say. But, there were two very distinct sides to his personality and he was masterful at hiding one of them in public.

∞ ∫ ∞

While we were in Canada, Raymond had been motivated by my older cousin's wife, Sue, to get fit again. She and my cousin used to jog every night and Raymond, being a former 'jock', was determined to regain his erstwhile athleticism when we returned to Australia. As with everything he did, he had to be seen as perfect in everyone's eyes. So, he went at it with a fury and determination that was a joy to behold, because he finally stopped drinking and was focussed on his fitness and developing his prowess as a triathlete. I learned as much as I could about nutrition and carb-loading for peak performance and became his support person, accompanying him to competitions all around Victoria.

Two years later, we returned to Canada where Raymond was scheduled to compete in various events in the Police and Fire Games. He came in the top 25% of the triathlete event and was very pleased. Unfortunately, he had put his hand up for the shot-put and failed, dismally. A colleague of his and I were watching and thought he would just laugh it off. But Raymond was humiliated. He genuinely believed everyone was laughing at him and he fell to pieces. Apparently, it was my fault! *Not again?* But, of course it was my fault. I was there to witness him making a fool of himself.

As soon as we were alone, out of sight of his colleague, he berated me, mercilessly, for laughing at him.

'But, surely Raymond, you could see the funny side of it,' I said. 'It's not as if you'd trained for the shot-put or that it was your main event. I think you were brave to even give it a go.'

Nothing would assuage his utter misery and when we returned to my cousin's house the atmosphere was tense. It was my turn to be embarrassed—I had brought this miasma of ill feeling into my hosts' house. It was my turn to feel dejected.

The next day was the swimming event and I did not go. When he returned, he was totally unhinged.

'I nearly drowned,' he bleated. Although he was a strong and graceful swimmer he apparently just gave up in mid-stroke.

'I wanted to win a medal for you, but you weren't there to support me.'

I learned later that he had won tons of medals, as a child and in his youth, and his father never had them engraved. He never showed any pride in his son and Raymond was hoping to get that admiration from me—the 'good' mother. I had failed him.

The following day, my youngest cousin took Raymond to a baseball game. We had delayed the celebration of our tenth anniversary until after the games, so I expected Raymond to come home to take me out to dinner. He didn't. Sue had lent him her car to ensure he would be back in plenty of time and I was worried he had had an accident. Finally, he arrived, falling over drunk, too late to go out.

All the work he had put in over the past two years was swept away. All the trust he had rebuilt with me was gone in that moment. Sue was understanding, but I was the 'burning-martyr'—having made the sacrifice of taking five weeks off from my post-graduate course to support him—and could not let it go. I was very demonstrative and threw him and his clothes out of our downstairs flat. I did not want to be associated with him and made a public display to convince everyone that his behaviour was unacceptable. No one else seemed to think it was a problem, but they didn't know our history.

∞ʃ∞

I feel ashamed of my behaviour because I have evolved psychologically since then. At the time, though, this was a response that came from the part of my subconscious that is my Raymond 'pain body'.[38]

∞ʃ∞

I wanted him as far away from me as possible and when he apologised, profusely, the next day I was unrelenting in my ire—that word my father used to use to formally express his anger with me. I wanted Raymond to feel as bad as I did, and I was succeeding.

He was resigned to fly back to Australia if I would not forgive him and I said, 'GO!'[39]

But Sue stepped in and placated me with, 'He just went on a bender to let off steam. Give him a break.'

I reluctantly acquiesced, and so we headed off on our driving adventure into the centre of British Columbia.

We stopped overnight at a B&B and I asked for a room with two beds. But, the next day, when we got to Sue's sister's house, there was a conspiracy to get us back together and her sister gave us her bedroom. Again, I found myself in a situation where my strong feelings of love and attachment overruled my resolve to end the relationship. I guess, in a way, I was as needy as Raymond. As always, his Don Juan[40] was able to mesmerise and seduce me.

∞ ∫ ∞

My conscious mind was happy and I forgave him—he loved me!

∞ ∫ ∞

We spent the next few days having a wonderful time and when we returned to my cousin's house we were, once more, the picture-perfect couple. We took off with Sue to explore Seattle for a couple of days and spent some time with other cousins on Vancouver Island. On our return, Sue's brother-in-law took us on his boat to a remote island and we set off to hike to the top of the mountain where there was a landmark called Beaver Dam.

Walking single file through the thicket I stepped awkwardly on a rock and went over on my ankle. I heard a loud crack and simultaneously experienced extreme pain. I passed out. When I came to, everyone was laughing. I had snapped the lateral ligament in my ankle. Raymond scooped me up in his arms, my knight[41]—the one and only time this archetype had manifested in our relationship—and carried me to the summit so I could see the dam. Then, he piggy-backed me all the way down the mountain and back to the boat. Everyone thought he was magnificent. He had redeemed himself. I was overjoyed!

He continued to be loving and supportive when we returned to Australia and had a meal prepared for me every night when I came home after a long day of work and then night school. I was lulled into a false sense of security—this behaviour would not last.

Things started to unravel again six months later, when I finished my post-graduate diploma and had started building my health promotion consultancy. I had restricted my previous career for ten years in favour of spending as much time with Raymond as his roster allowed. But now I was less flexible as I had to fulfil contracts to deliver workshops whenever they were scheduled by my service providers. This meant having to be away from Raymond on evenings we usually spent together. Even though I would share my experiences with him, he didn't share the joy I was deriving from interacting with workshop participants. While he didn't say anything, his body reacted.

Raymond's first and second chakra energies were severely depleted by his deprived childhood. These chakras are related to tribal power and the power of relationships, respectively.[42] The physical manifestations are—amongst other ailments—chronic lower back pain and sciatica. Consequently, Raymond had suffered from crippling back pain all his life, which periodically incapacitated him. Each time he had an episode I would chauffeur him back and forth between his sport's medicine physician and his physiotherapist. I believe his episodes were more extreme because of the anger he would attach to them—the abandoned child separated from his tribe.

As always happened, he found someone or something to blame for these episodes. However, this time was different. He withdrew from all physical contact with me and after three months I experienced a psychic breakdown. I could no longer cope with his aggression and his return to drinking—he said he drank to ease the pain. He also stopped his triathlon training and competing, which he blamed on his back. As was his pattern, his Shadow Saboteur[43] manifested itself.

My emotions had gone through so many upheavals and my trust had been broken on so many occasions that I withdrew. I began my Master's degree in health science and within two years my part-time

consultancy was thriving. I had left my secure employ-
ment as a scientist/lecturer and developed a full-time
health promotion business. But things did not go as
smoothly as I had hoped, due to government cutbacks
to not-for-profit organisations that were my clients. I
was floundering—financially and spiritually—and no
one was there to rescue me.

Raymond had been elected to the Metropol-
itan Fire Brigade Union Branch Committee and
was putting all his energy into fighting 'The Estab-
lishment'—a fight his Shadow Rebel gloried in. He
would come home with a harrowing story of how
'they are trying to destroy us'. He talked ad nauseum
about a female committee member, Loz—short for
Lauren—how great she was, how feisty. 'She reminds
me of you when you were younger,' he said. All his
libidinal energy was consumed by the committee—or
so I thought—and he became emotionally unavailable
to me. He physically detached and we had no sex-life.
If it wasn't a backache, he was too tired. Whenever I
made romantic advances he would get angry and start
an argument.

One day I had had enough. He was away on a
strategic Branch Committee retreat when my hot
water service sprang a leak. It was in the ceiling, so my
entrance hallway was flooded. I switched on the light
and it arced. I was worried it might have started a fire
and so I called the fire brigade. The firefighters arrived
and ripped down the ceiling to make sure there were
no spot fires.

This couldn't have happened at a worse time for me. The next day I had to counsel two senior personnel in regional Victoria whose positions had been made redundant, and I had to prepare their outplacement manuals and other resources for career transition. It was freezing cold and I could not use the ducted heating or make a cup of tea or have a shower.

The 'boys' (fire-fighters) cut me some wood for the stove heater and invited me to their fire station to have a shower. One of them recognised me and asked where Raymond was and why he hadn't cut some wood for me.

'He's off fighting the good fight for you blokes,' I said. They weren't impressed.

The insurance assessor kindly offered to photocopy the resource materials for me and I held it all together, with his support. My Warrior was manifesting as stoicism and giving me the strength of will that I needed to do this. I held my emotions in check and managed to assuage the angst of both clients who had lost their jobs after many years of service and dedication.

When I returned home I found that Raymond was not there yet. He had left a phone message to say he was too tired and would see me in the morning. He arrived the next day, full of praise for Loz, the fantastic camaraderie they had experienced and how wonderful … yada, yada … blah, blah!

'Well, this is how it was for me.' I told him my story and there was a protracted silence. He looked sheepish and lost for words.

'And you know something, Raymond? I managed to hold it all together without you. So, I started to think, what's the point? You are never there for me anymore. You give all your energy to the Branch Committee and that's where you seem to be most fulfilled. We have no love life, no intimacy and no future plans together. What say we end it now and avoid any more suffering? Go away, Raymond, just go away.'

He wasn't prepared for this and couldn't even muster an angry response. But then he said, unexpectedly, 'I realised when I was away how much you mean to me. You are the most important thing in my life. I'll do anything you ask.'

'Why should I believe you?'

'Just give me one more chance. I want to spend *forever* with you.'

And I did. What was wrong with me?

This pattern of giving in, relenting, forgiving, was such a self-destructive way to be. But, I was totally unaware of the underlying forces that kept me stuck. It would be years before I would be able to break out of this pattern and, with this awareness, start on the road to enlightenment. But there had to be a tsunami! As Jung said, 'The falling apart releases the energy necessary for the creation of new structures'.[44]

I thought this was a new beginning. Raymond started to talk about moving in together and we planned to sell both houses. We began looking for a place where we could still have our own space and found the perfect house on a large property in Kangaroo Ground. We made an offer and left to drive to Newcastle, where I was attending a conference.

The drive stirred up Raymond's back problems and he complained, endlessly. He blamed me for choosing to take my car instead of his, 'If you'd have let me drive my car, I wouldn't have this pain'. The pattern had returned.

When we came home and were in the final stages of buying the property, Raymond said he would handle the negotiations. On the phone call to the agent he sabotaged the deal by becoming abusive and calling the agent a 'horse-trader'. I was left despondent when he hung up the phone, turned to me and said, 'Well, there's no way I can maintain that huge property now that my back's fucked.'

I was made to feel that it was my fault and there was no more discussion about looking for another property.

It was shortly after this incident, that I had a car accident and sustained a whiplash injury. I was in a lot of pain and distress. I could not work, and my business started to fail. Life had become intolerable but, somehow, I got through with a lot of psychological counselling.

With our plans to buy a house together abandoned and our energy drained from the physical pain we were both in, our relationship had fallen into a slump—something was needed to reinvigorate it. And so, I conceived a plan to get us working on a project together …

Raymond's 45th birthday was coming up and I suggested we have a barbeque and invite all his colleagues from the Branch Committee, his brother, Kyle, and his only friend, Clive. Raymond threw himself into the party arrangements and it proved to be a good diversion. Over the weeks of preparation, a closeness returned between us. However, two days before the event, he was offered a spinal-block day-procedure and he opted to go into hospital rather than postpone until after the party. When he came home he reverted to his angry persona.

The day of the party was fraught with tension, as the weather had turned, and rain threatened. Raymond was slinging a canopy across the yard and, when I came out to make a suggestion, he said, 'You're the cunt who made me do this so just fuck off inside!' To say I was devastated is an understatement. What's more, he said it in front of Kyle.

That evening, I avoided him and mingled with the guests. It was the first time I had met his colleagues from the Branch Committee. Loz had brought me flowers and they all said how they were so pleased to meet me after all the glowing comments that Raymond had made about me. I was dumbfounded—if only they knew how he had treated me that very morning.

Later that evening, Raymond made his birthday speech. He began by thanking his brother, then his mate, Clive, and then named all the members of the Branch Committee. Eventually he said, 'And I want to thank the 'love of my life' for everything she has done for me in the past 18 years. Without her, I would not be alive today.'

I was stunned, and it obviously showed on my face, because I just stared back with a look of what I imagine was total amazement. The hypocrisy was staggering. I could not buy into this show that he was putting on for his audience.

After I cleaned up the remnants of the festivities, I drove home and left Raymond to 'have a drink' with some mates I had never met, who had turned up uninvited after everyone had left. When he arrived at my place, the next day, it was as if nothing had happened. There was no discussion of the episode—his other persona had come to the fore. But I was emotionally detached and going through the motions of being in a couple. Something needed to change.

It would be two more years before I decided to take a stand and once again broach the subject of our living arrangements with Raymond. I figured that if we had a house together, we could regain the emotional closeness that I craved—the Child: Magical still believed that anything was possible.

Where Did Forever Go?

I felt the trust
disintegrate –
watched the loving die –
did you ever really love me –
or was your love
a lovely lie …

Nan Witcomb,
The Thoughts of Nanushka, Vol 12:
Tears and Tenderness

Finally, I bit the bullet and sold my home—I figured that twenty years was a long time to invest in a
relationship and I still believed we could turn things
around and make lasting positive changes. I told Raymond that I would be moving into his house tempo-
rarily, and then we could focus on finding a new place
where we could live together. He didn't put up any
resistance or get angry. I supposed that he was mel-
lowing and could see the sense in this.

Raymond insisted on carrying me across the
threshold of his house after loading and then unload-
ing a semitrailer of my furniture. It was so romantic.
He said his back was bad, so I didn't baulk when he
said he needed a beer to ease the pain. This was his
panacea for all that ailed him.

But, it didn't stop there. Every night he drank. I dared not say anything because I felt guilty—it was my fault his back hurt. After all, he had martyred[45] himself for me. This was a pattern that had been playing out for years. I did not have the courage to mention it had been his choice to do the heavy lifting that the house-move required.

A week later it was his best mate, Clive's, birthday. He told me that he was going to have one final drink. A 'drink' to Raymond meant getting paralytic. But this would be the last time and then he was going to commit himself to making a life for us in his, and my, new home. At least that's what he said.

When we got to the party I was quickly abandoned while he caught up with everyone from his past.

'You understand, love. These are people I haven't seen for a long time.'

I tried to make conversation but didn't know anyone except the hosts. And they were busy serving their guests.

After the food and speeches, I asked if we could go. Raymond was falling-over drunk and took a great deal of time saying goodbye, even though most guests had left. When we had driven some distance from the venue he said, 'Ya know? I wanted to stay.' I immediately turned back and dropped him off without uttering a word.

He did not come home that night. He did not come home the next morning. He didn't call. Nobody called. I cried thinking that something had happened to him. Eventually, he came home towards evening, unapologetic, angry and distant. I was devastated. What had happened to the dream?

I blocked out the conscious pain, but I think it got stored in my subconscious and added itself to the mistrust of 'his word'. Things got worse and the atmosphere was pregnant with foreboding. What had I done? I felt trapped. I had no means of escape. Nowhere to go. It was like being oppressed—me: the independent, self-sufficient woman who had influenced younger female scientists to assert themselves in the workplace. Again, I withdrew, hoping this would pass and that we would get back to being lovers and friends again.

∞∫∞

I remember going to an event a week later—that my brother Michael had organised—and remonstrating about how disillusioned I felt and that I wanted to move out. His friends, who knew me well, thought I was being funny; but I was serious. What had come over Raymond? Why was he behaving like an adolescent? What could I do? I just did what I always do—I withdrew.

∞∫∞

Over the following months Raymond's behaviour became more and more erratic, one moment aggressive the next withdrawn. He refused to engage with me and went away 'camping' at every opportunity. I did not know what to do and, because I had been disabled with spinal pain since the car accident two years earlier, I was unable to earn a reliable income, so felt I couldn't move out. It was I who was needy now—physically and emotionally. But, there was no comfort coming from Raymond. And, once again, I felt totally alone.

But then I started to fight back—aggression with aggression. What was happening to me? I hated this person I was becoming. His response was to act like a wounded child and then the 'good' mother would feel sorry and relent.

But, the 'good' mother had burned out.

Revelations of Psychotherapy

Did you ever
really care for me –
or was it
just 'pretend' –
I dare not ask
for fear
you'll kill my dream
of the beginning –
and leave me
with my nightmare
of the end –

Nan Witcomb,
The Thoughts of Nanushka, Vol 11:
Gift of Love

Moving in with Raymond proved to be his breaking point. Although I was made to feel as though I was invading his space and trespassing on his freedom, it was the fact that the dynamics had changed. While I believed that we could have an adult–adult relationship, Raymond was unable to.

I had been perceived as the 'good' mother up to the point when I moved in with him. I had nurtured his orphan Child 'self' and tolerated his rebellious and free-spirited—*let's see how far I can push the boundaries*—adolescent 'self'. Expecting him to start acting like an adult was tantamount to abandoning him. This certainly explains why he was continuously angry and had started to drink more frequently.

Now it was me who had to break away from being the nurturing, caring, unconditionally-loving person. All the love I had to give, I couldn't give it to the person I loved. Hence, I was in conflict, wanting to love and be with Raymond, and knowing that he was now beyond my reach. What I didn't know was that he had attached to another 'good' mother.

It later came to light, that Raymond had spent his 'camping' trips forging a co-dependent relationship with his stepbrother, Josh's, wife.

Gerry, his full brother in Western Australia, made me see another dimension of that relationship. He said that Raymond had told him years before that he would leave me if I ever wanted children because he did not want the responsibility. A lesson well learnt from his parents. Playing Uncle Raymond was a way he could have the children and no responsibility.

Raymond had compartmentalised the life he had with her and his nephews and had continued to share a life with me—he could have his cake and eat it too. While this worked when I lived in a separate house, the additional energy he had to put into juggling these separate parts of himself caused an upheaval that he could not cope with psychologically. And so, he moved out. He chose her—it was easier for him.

For me, the physical and emotional pain was

unbearable. Metaphorically, I imagined it was like losing a child at birth—as though my breasts were full of milk and the child I had been nurturing had suddenly died. I felt as if I was going to burst if I couldn't give him my love and that drove me to continue to contact him and want to be with him.

Finally, it all came together for me. When I thought back to what may have triggered his feeling that I had abandoned him as the 'good' mother, it was all so clear. It was the night of his 45th birthday party. In his eyes, he had opened his heart for all to see and I had rejected him. He seemed oblivious of the way he had treated me and the anger he had acted-out towards me, in front of his brother, as we were preparing for the party. I behaved the way I felt—dazed. It was from that moment that he seemed to withdraw. I remember him saying to me in an almost childlike, pathetic way, 'Now that I have declared my love, you treat me as if it doesn't matter.' Just like the long-lost mother he strove to find and who only cared about Kyle.

Declaring his love was the most trusting thing he had ever done, whereas for me to say 'I love you' came naturally—I said it often; and meant it. I did not know at the time how profound that admission was for him and that he could compartmentalise his angry treatment of me during the day from his loving gesture in front of his friends.

We were in a co-dependent relationship—Raymond's neediness for love and my need to give it.

Damaged people don't let you in, because they are so untrusting. When Raymond finally declared his love for me, I somehow disappointed him because I did not respond in the way he expected.

He was not aware that he had battered me all day with his anger. He compartmentalised that part of his behaviour and kept it separate to the 'here and now'. I'd let him down. That's all his abandoned Child could understand. That was the point at which his subconscious started to accumulate evidence that I was, in fact, the 'bad' mother—worthy only of scorn.

I couldn't blame him for what he had done. It was a survival mechanism. Compartmentalising, duplicity and manipulation—to protect and mask his hurt 'self'—were the art of survival for him. Hence the shadow attribute of the Bully:[46] his abuse of me, and of the Hero:[47] his perceived rescuing of his brother's wife and family.

I am now wiser. I must fight the guilt I feel for his perception that I abandoned him. Strangely, I don't hate him. But I know that I don't want to be with him. It would destroy me and I'm worth more than that.

Settlement

I never did stop
loving **you** –
only what you have
become –

Nan Witcomb,
The Thoughts of Nanushka, Vol 5:
Pocketful of Dreams

After Raymond left, I spent the most miserable time
of my life grieving. I was sick at heart and couldn't
see a way out of the darkness. In my family of origin,
I was the one who'd always subsumed my needs and
wants for those of my parents and siblings. I then did
it with Gray and later with Raymond.[48]

When I finally let my family's needs come second
to mine, they discarded me.[49] It was now time to put
myself first. But I had to learn to do that. People who
work in a 'giving' profession need to give of themselves. Raymond had gutted me and I had nothing
left to give. I lost interest in my work, which had been
the only thing sustaining me. I found myself unable to
make an income because I was in mourning. I had sunk
to the lowest level of Maslow's Hierarchy of Needs.

I had been living off my cashed-in assets after the
car accident. It merely sustained me. I needed to give

myself permission to use the ammunition I had at my disposal to make sure I secured a favourable financial settlement. It did not matter whether Raymond thought badly of me. I really had nothing to lose.

I also had to learn to hate him. Because I loved him, I was suffering more. 'That's why divorces are so acrimonious; the couple have to hate each other to get through the emotional pain,' I was told by my counsellor. We weren't officially married, but the pain was no less intense.

Journey out of
the Darkness of Grief

I remember nights
when a lazy sea
lapped gently on silver sand –
I remember me,
brown and salty,
still warm from the morning sun,
drunk with living
and loving life
with a passionate innocence
which has never really left me …

Nan Witcomb,
The Thoughts of Nanushka, Vol 5:
Pocketful of Dreams

I did not want to hate Raymond, although I hated what he did. Hatred and anger only embitter and destroy us.

Carolyn Myss says that, 'When a person breaks his word [and let's face it, Raymond did that repeatedly] that action reverberates for years within the psyche of the betrayed. It cuts to the soul'. My fifth chakra had been controlled by others' expectations of me and I suffered deeply because of that. It was time to take control and I needed to draw on 'the inherent knowledge of the fifth chakra [and] develop the strength to make choices which reflected who I [was]'.[50]

I decided that I required guidance to light my way through this maze, to find a newer stronger 'self'. I consulted the *Sacred Contract* Archetypes[51] and started to choose those attributes that would enable me to heal, grow and move on.

The first one I chose was *The Goddess*. This archetype represents the feminine expressed through wisdom, life force and sensuality. She made me love my body and myself again—or for the first time. I started a fitness regime, lost excess weight and re-established a healthy lifestyle.

The Damsel revealed to me the nature of healthy romance and empowered me to take care of myself.

The Femme Fatale released my erotic energy and opened my heart to love. I was able to fall in love again a year later. And, when I realised I was in another mother–child relationship, I knew it and I was okay with releasing it. I am now happy in my own skin and complete within myself. I feel no need to be in a couple—I live in positive solitude.

The Child: Eternal keeps me young in mind, body and spirit and enables me to see life and love with fresh eyes. I have embarked on many adventures and found the vigour to write, make new friends and push the boundaries: travelling extensively and embarking on professionally creative projects. My resilience knows no bounds. I rise like a phoenix from the ashes whenever I am faced with an existential crisis—I have bounced back from several health predicaments, professional disappointments and personal frustrations.

The Storyteller motivated me to tell my story—disclosing all my foolishness, mistakes, successes and acquired wisdom.

The Gossip has empowered me to pass on private information that I have long held in trust. It has been detrimental to my wellbeing to keep this information confidential, and now my story may release others from abusive relationships.

The Exorcist has freed me from the destructive impulses of others and inspired me to influence clients to let go of their negative spirits. I have become a mentor to others and coach them to build a positive self-image.

The Destroyer has enabled me to release limiting self-beliefs and thereby prepared me for a new life of self-determination and empowerment. My closest friends are positive people who are supportive and life affirming.

The Avenger has imbued in me the desire to balance the scales of justice and it has served me well when negotiating a fair financial settlement with Raymond—something I failed to do when I divorced Gray. It has guarded me against people who would take financial advantage of me, and now I stand my ground for what is fair.

The Healer has reconnected me with my innate talent for helping others repair their mind and spirit.

I lost my compassion for those in need of healing but, by embracing the energy of this archetype, I can now pass this energy on to others.

The Child: Wounded has permitted me to un-lock the memories of abuse, neglect and other traumas that I experienced in childhood. It has opened my eyes to the fact that all the years that I stayed with Raymond were due to a sense of compassion and desire to nurture a wounded child, while sublimating my own need to be healed. It has encouraged me to forgive him and continue to assist other wounded children—but not at my expense! I now know how to set boundaries with people who are Emotional Vampires.[52]

The Virgin has given me symbolic purity of heart and spirit and reinvigorated me to create a new beginning, a new 'self', and to birth new ideas. I have taken this creativity into my business and now train people to embrace new ways to relate to others.

The Networker provides the impetus to pass on this information to those who find themselves abandoned. I hope in sharing my story, they will find the strength to leave abusive relationships, love themselves and still feel compassion for those who abandoned them. I do.

Author's After Note – Nature or Nurture?

It is interesting to consider that, as a child, Anne was traumatised, neglected, exploited and humiliated; as Raymond was. And yet, she did not become duplicitous, develop self-harming habits or take her anger out on others.

Perhaps her choice to connect with the Light side of her governing archetypes was a determining factor in shaping her response to the tragedies she experienced.

Maybe being in a family—albeit, as the one who dared to exercise her independence and free herself of playing the roles that accommodated the needs of her family—enabled her to develop strengths of her tribal/first chakra, such as identity, bonding, a feeling of security and of connectedness to the world. Whereas without a family, Raymond had developed tribal chakra insecurities, such as feelings of abandonment and fears for his physical survival.

She says that despite the neglect and exploitation by her parents and siblings she did feel loved. She attributes her capacity to love others to her governing archetypes, which imbued her with empathy and a nurturing predisposition.

Anne believes her 'sacred contract' was to influence Raymond to develop a conscience and to feel remorse for how cruelly he treated her.

His parting words to her were, 'I feel we are going to be together again, someday.' Maybe he also believed that they were *be'shert*.

About the Author

Cecile Ravell is a creative memoir writer who is inspired by her observations as a psychotherapist and student of human behaviour. She is a proponent of *writing as therapy* and has seen, first hand, how drawing on the strengths of Jungian Archetypes can help people move on from loss.

Cecile is the author of *Child Magical – a memoir* and *Dilemmas of a Middle-aged Madonna*. Chapters from each of these stories have been published in two Anthologies—*Literary Allsorts* and *Ties that Bind*. Her fascination with innate personality temperament combined with her passion for travel, enable her to take the female protagonists on an internal as well as external journey of discovery.

Endnotes

Author's Introduction – The Perennial Question

[1] C.S. Jung postulated the existence of a collective unconscious, which he says is inherited and is made up essentially of archetypes. *The Portable Jung*, C.S. p60

Kismet

[2] Raymond's Shadow Vampire formed a psychic attachment to me out of desire for approval and sustenance. He played the Victim to get sympathy as a form of positive feedback. *Sacred Contracts* pp 412 & 413.

[3] Don Juan, Shadow: uses the power of romantic attraction for private agendas. *Sacred Contracts* p380

[4] Lover, Light attributes: great passion and devotion. Unbridled appreciation of something or someone. *Sacred Contracts* p392

[5] Lover, Shadow: self-destructive devotion. *Sacred Contracts* p392

Early Days – Early Warning Signals

[6] Child: Orphan, Light attribute: independence based on learning to go it alone and conquering the fear of survival. Child: Orphan, Shadow: feelings of abandonment that stifle maturation. The abandoned child seeks inappropriate surrogate families. *Sacred Contracts* p372

[7] Mother, Light attribute: patience, nurturance and unconditional love. *Sacred Contracts* p396

[8] 'Adult Attachment Processes: Individual and Couple Perspectives', Bartholomew, K. *British Journal of Medical Psychology,* 1997, 70: 249–253

[9] Lover, Shadow: self-destructive devotion. *Sacred Contracts* p392

[10] Hedonist, Shadow: pursues pleasure to the detriment of health and indulges at the expense of others. *Sacred Contracts* p387

[11] Trickster, Shadow: manipulates others through duplicity. *Sacred Contracts* p411

[12] Addict, Shadow: allows an addictive pattern to have authority over his inner spirit. *Sacred Contracts* p364

[13] Child: Magical, Light attribute: sees the potential for sacred beauty in all things. *Sacred Contracts* p373

[14] *Families and How to Survive Them*, Skinner, R and Cleese, J. pp17-19

My Story – Child: Magical

[15] Rebel, Light attribute: breaking away from cultural patterns. *Sacred Contracts* p403

[16] Victim, Light attribute: prevents you from letting yourself be victimised, or victimising others. *Sacred Contracts* p413

[17] Prostitute, Light attribute: accentuates the challenge of surviving without negotiating the power of your spirit. *Sacred Contracts* p402

[18] Warrior, Light attribute: confers the ability to protect and fight for your rights. *Sacred Contracts* p414

[19] Angel, Light attribute: helps those in need with no expectation of return. *Sacred Contracts* p367

[20] Rescuer, Light attributes: provides strength and support to others in crisis. Acts out of love with no expectation of reward. *Sacred Contracts* p404

21 Teacher, Light attribute: able to communicate knowledge, experience, skill or wisdom. *Sacred Contracts* p219

22 Liberator, Light attributes: freeing oneself from outmoded beliefs. Releasing negative thought patterns. *Sacred Contracts* p391

23 Warrior, Light attributes: strength, skill, discipline and toughness of will. *Sacred Contracts* p414

24 Visionary, Light attributes: capacity to envision what is not yet conceivable to others. Willing to proclaim a vision without regard for personal gain. *Sacred Contracts* p414

25 Be'shert: Yiddish for 'destined to be your beloved'. *Sacred Contracts*

Raymond's Story – Child: Orphan

26 Bully, Light attributes: Helps confront fears that bully you. Takes on those who bully others. *Sacred Contracts* p371

27 Bully, Shadow: conceals deep fears – of true identity being found out – behind verbal or physical abuse. *Sacred Contracts* p371

28   Hero, Shadow: escapism and a false sense of hero-ism. *Sacred Contracts* p388

29   Hero, Light attribute: confronting survival fears which would compromise his journey of personal empowerment. *Sacred Contracts* p388

Our Story – Star-Crossed Lovers

30   *Oliver Twist*, Dickens, Charles.

31   Child: Magical, Light attributes: gifted with imagination and the belief that everything is possible. *Sacred Contracts* p373

32   Angel, Light attribute: having a loving and nurturing character. *Sacred Contracts* p367

33   Mother, Light attributes: shows nurturance, patience and unconditional love. *Sacred Contracts* p396

34   Teacher, Light attribute: may manifest through wisdom and guidance … or by inspired instruction in spirituality. *Sacred Contracts* p219

35   Hedonist, Shadow: pursues pleasure without regard for other people or one's own health and wellbeing. *Sacred Contracts* p387

36 Bully, Shadow: gives in to fear by lashing out – bullying others. *Sacred Contracts* p371

37 Trickster, Shadow: manipulates others through duplicity. *Sacred Contracts* p411

38 *A New Earth*, Tolle, Eckart. Ch 5

39 Mother, Shadow: abandoning. *Sacred Contracts* p396

40 Don Juan, Shadow: uses the power of romantic attraction for private agendas. *Sacred Contracts* p380

41 Knight, Light attribute: protects the princess. *Sacred Contracts* p390

42 *Anatomy of Spirit* pp103 & 129

43 Saboteur, Shadow: self-destructive behavior. *Sacred Contracts* p405

44 *Modern Man in Search of a Soul*, Jung, C.G. p70

Where Did Forever Go?

45 The Martyr Archetype sacrifices himself for others. But this was the Shadow side – he utilised a combination of service (moving my furniture)

and suffering (the perennial bad back) as a means of controlling and manipulating me (making me feel guilty). *Sacred Contracts* p392

Revelations of Psychotherapy

[46] Bully, Shadow: conceals deep fears behind verbal and physical abuse. *Sacred Contracts* p371

[47] Hero, Shadow: escapism and a false sense of hero-ism. *Sacred Contracts* p388

Settlement

[48] Slave, Shadow: lacks the power of choice and self-authority and is manipulated by others. *Sacred Contracts* p408

[49] *Families and How to Survive Them*, Skinner, R and Cleese, J. p18

Journey out of the Darkness of Grief

[50] *Sacred Contracts* p179

[51] *Sacred Contracts* pp384, 377, 382, 374, 409, 385, 381, 378, 370, 386, 373, 413, 398

[52] *Emotional Vampires: Dealing with People Who Drain You Dry*, Bernstein, Albert J.

Bibliography

Bartholomew, K. 'Adult Attachment Processes: Individual and Couple Perspectives', *British Journal of Medical Psychology*, 1997, 70: 249–253

Bernstein, Albert J. *Emotional Vampires: Dealing with People Who Drain You Dry*, McGraw-Hill Professional 2012

Dickens, Charles. *Oliver Twist*, 1838

Jung, C.S. *The Portable Jung*, Translated by Hull, R.F.C. Penguin 1977

Jung, C.G. *Modern Man in Search of a Soul,* Harcourt Inc. 1933 p70

Maslow, Abraham. *A Theory of Human Motivation*, Psychological Review 1943

Myss, Caroline. *The Anatomy of Spirit,* Bantam Books Transworld Publishers (Aust) Pty Ltd. 1997

Myss, Caroline. *Sacred Contracts*, Bantam Books Transworld Publishers (Aust) Pty Ltd. 2001

Skinner, R. and Cleese, J. *Families and How to Survive Them*, Vermillion 1997

Tolle, Eckart. *A New Earth*, PLUME Publ. 2008

Witcomb, Nan. *The Thoughts of Nanushka, Vol 11: Gift of Love,* ©Nan Witcomb – nanushka@senet.com.au, 1985.

Witcomb, Nan. *The Thoughts of Nanushka, Vol 12: Tears and Tenderness*, ©Nan Witcomb – nanushka@senet.com.au, 1985

Witcomb, Nan. *The Thoughts of Nanushka, Vol 5: Pocketful of Dreams*, ©Nan Witcomb – nanushka@senet.com.au, 1976

www.ingramcontent.com/pod-product-compliance
Lightning Source LLC
Chambersburg PA
CBHW032150020426
42334CB00016B/1263